Hailey Goes Testing

Marcus builds a boat

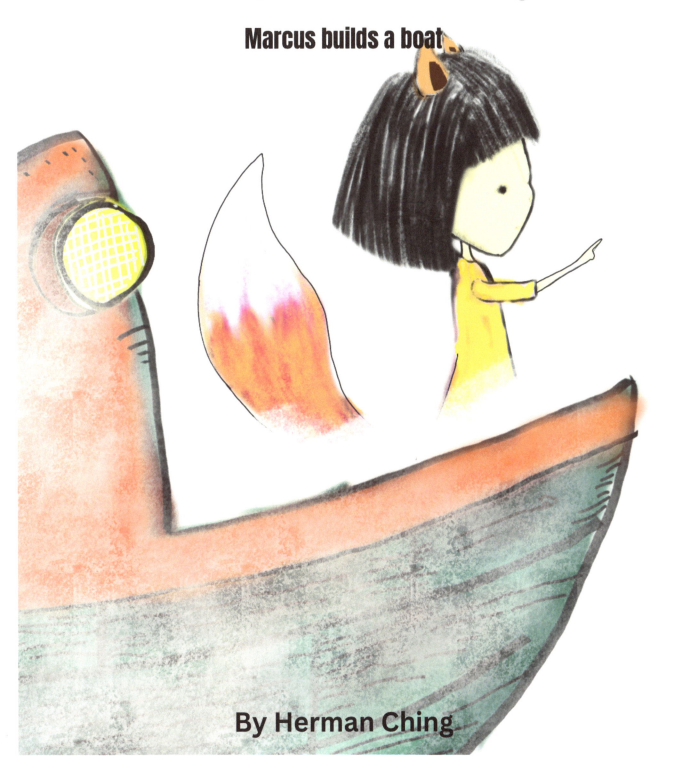

By Herman Ching

INSPIRATION

I wanted to create stories about testing.
Testing has so many
dimensions. I wanted to inspire the young
generation in an ever changing world the
ideas about testing. I hope that through this
book and hopefully more that could be
possible. Thank you for reading and for
your patronage.

- Herman Ching

Version: 1.0.1
Branch: Testing

This is Hailey. She wants to be a tester like her Daddy.

This is Marcus. He likes to build. He built a boat.

Hailey saw it and asked can she test his boat. Marcus said yes.

Hailey asked Marcus some questions about the boat.

With her curious mind, Hailey went off to test the boat.

She filled the tub with water and put the boat right on the water.

It sank!

Hailey told him what happened and how Marcus can see the same result.

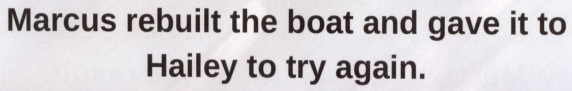

Marcus rebuilt the boat and gave it to Hailey to try again.

It floats!

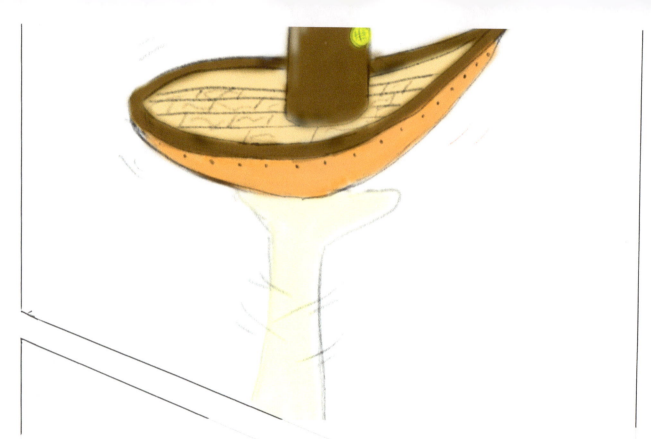

Hailey threw the boat into water as hard as she could.

It still floats!

Hailey made big waves around the boat.
Marcus covered his eyes.

It still floats!

Hailey tries another test. She puts one rubber ducky on the boat.

Hailey puts two rubber duckies on the boat.

Hailey puts three rubber duckies.

One fell off.

1. This boat can still float when I threw in the tub.
2. This boat can still float in very high waves
3. This boat can hold two rubber duckies.

— Hailey

Hailey went to Marcus to tell him what she has learned.

"Here you go Marcus, it is a great boat"

Marcus gleamed and said to Hailey,
"Thanks for testing the boat."

"I made this boat for you. Here you go. You are going to be a great tester one day."